Another Month

That Matters

31 Evangelical Essays and Prayers

L. R. Abbott

Introduction

If you have read <u>A Month That Matters</u>, you have a good idea what to expect as you go on to read, <u>Another Month That Matters</u>. Here again you will meet people, go places and, in your mind's eye, sometimes walk in the shoes of others. In Psalm 119:30 God declares, "The entrance of My Word brings light." That inner illumination of spiritual truths found in the Bible are what I aimed for in writing these essays. In many ways each is a parable, "an earthly story with heavenly meaning." While parables are most often thought of as coming from the pages of Scripture, they are also found in my life and yours when we see our lives though the prism of God's Word. Such is the belief that formed the content of this book.

The idea is to read one essay for each day of any one month of the year you choose. While you may not look up each of all the Scripture references throughout, I hope you may do so when you want more information about what is said, or aren't certain why I said it. The verse references are there, not to weigh you down in your reading, but to assist you as you desire.

May you read and be blessed as you have for yourself, <u>Another Month That Matters</u>!

CONTENTS

"Endeavor to keep the unity of the Spirit in the bond of peace."

My first paying job as a junior high school student was working as a closing dishwasher at a hometown diner. One night the owner's son showed up with a friend. Together they thought it equally enjoyable to stage a kitchen knife fight. Their play escalated in aggressiveness to where their arm motions grew wild and, despite my appeals for them to stop, the sharp edge of the owner's son's knife nearly severed a finger off the hand of his friend. It was at that moment the father appeared on the scene. Obviously dismayed by what he saw, he quickly escorted the injured boy to the hospital. I, on the other hand, had more to clean up than just dishes.

Objects with sharp edges, like swords, knives, and blades of all sorts, must be handled with respect if injury of one kind or another is to be avoided. Similarly, the Sword of the Spirit, which is the Word of God, must be handled with respect. Hebrews 4:12 says it is, "sharper than any two-edged sword, cutting between the soul and spirit, between joint and marrow. It exposes our innermost thoughts and desires."

While the use of God's Word is normally considered to be a good thing which benefits hearers,[1] sharing it must be accompanied by the handler having respect and love for his hearer.[2] How many times has a believer "faced off" over a perceived Scriptural difference of doctrinal opinion, only to "pierce and thrust" back and forth at another individual using God's sharp sword? Too often the result of this for one or both persons is hurt feelings, disrupted fellowship, and loss of peace. Sadly, the occasioned difference between them is usually a secondary matter about which sincere Christians sometimes disagree. Such things need not give otherwise agreeable people reason to aggressively escalate their sword's use towards their neighbor. After all, it may be that one or the other, or even both individuals, might have some spiritual growing up to do before seeing things as a friend does,[4] and spiritual sword fighting will do little to aid the process of anyone's spiritual illumination. The fact is, a person who is under attack feels himself forced to go on the defensive and the result is their ears close.

Love and respect for the Word of God and those we share God's Word with... this is what will insure the power wielded behind the Christian's sword is under God's control and not their own. Our undisciplined actions will fail to yield the "peaceable fruit"[5] we desire and, at the conclusion of any Scriptural debate, the last thing we want is for someone to have to make a trip to the hospital!

*Lord, help me to share with love and respect
what you have taught me from your Word.*

1) Romans 10:17

2) Philemon 1:6

3) Galatians 5:13-15

4) 1 Corinthians 8:11

5) Hebrews 12:11-13

"I will remember my covenant, which is between
me and you and every living creature."

People's curiosity about wild animals has often gotten them into trouble. If it is not happening by their getting too close to animals in their natural habitat, it is happening when they bring them home to an unnatural one. Consider the precarious love affair some backyard owners of exotic animals have had...

In Texas a four year old was injured by his aunt's pet cougar. In Connecticut, a 55 year old woman was disfigured by her friend's pet chimpanzee. In Ohio a 200 pound kangaroo attacked an 80 year old man and, in Nebraska, a 34 year old man was strangled by his pet snake. Then too, in 2011, one man in Ohio released fifty of his animals, among them lions, tigers and bears. After letting them go, he committed suicide, leaving other people to deal with the problem. They did. Local officials had no choice but to shoot and kill all the creatures because of the immediate public safety threat they posed.

How different the future will be for peoples' relationships with wild animals when God establishes His new world order![1] The new natures of both man and animals will at that time allow them to live together in peaceful, safe relationship.[2] This truth that the animals have a future presence on earth in the permanent, heavenly state of resurrected people on earth, is entirely in keeping with God's covenant promises to Noah in Genesis 9:9-17. There, God repeatedly emphasizes He will preserve, not only wild animals forever, but He will also do it along with "every living creature of every kind."

In the glorious future of Christ's ruling on earth,[3] the wild natures of both animals and man will have reverted to what they were before the fall. Before sin and its accompanying judgment, the unfallen nature of both animals and man posed no danger to one another. This is why in the new earth a child may escort animals such as wolfs, leopards and lions with no threat of danger.[4] They will even play with cobras and vipers without injurious consequence.[5]

Just think, in 2011 there were 2000 dangerous incidents with exotic animals across the United States, yet throughout eternity in the new heavens and earth there will be none! For the lack of understanding Biblical teaching on this subject, or the lack of faith to believe it, many people fail to appreciate this truth. Wouldn't it be great if those wishing to now own exotic animals believed this? If they did, they might be willing to wait a little while in order to have the wonderful and safe relationship with all animals God plans to provide.[6]

Lord, help me respect all the wonderful animals you have created.
Thank you that when you restore all things animals will be included.

1) Revelation 21:1-3

2) Revelation 21:4

3) Revelation 11:15

4) Isaiah 11:6

5) Isaiah 11:8

6) Revelation 21:4

"Peter then denied again; and immediately a rooster crowed."

How would you like to be awakened each morning by a rooster crowing three feet from your head? I didn't. That was my situation when a rooster I owned decided to make his early, new day announcements just the other side of a windowed wall where I soundly slept. His persistence at this continued unabated until the day he became the main focus at our family dinner table. Following his absence, I enjoyed being awakened by an alarm clock... the time, volume and distance from which, unlike the rooster, I could control.

There was a rooster in the life of the apostle Peter that he could not control, but God certainly did. Just as Christ said would be the case,[1] that rooster crowed immediately after Peter denied Christ a third time. Talk about a wake-up call! By this, Peter's better senses were awakened, moving him to weep bitterly[2] over what he had done.

New days are gifts from a loving God, so are wake up calls. A deeper experience with Him is often preceded by our becoming aware we have behaved in a manner inconsistent with our relationship to Jesus. This is what happened to Peter. His words and behavior denied the vital relationship with Christ that was his calling.[3] Similarly, as Christ followers, we too can expect God to give us a wake-up call when we have behaved badly. The loss of peace and joy that accompanies our failure alerts us to our need of repentance. God will help us get our repentance right. It may not be easy but, as with Peter, the Lord will gently draw us back to Himself.[4] As a result, He restores our fellowship and usefulness to Him, our joy and peace returns.[5]

There is always the possibility of hearing your own "rooster's crow." As often as it may happen, see it as a gracious act of God, a divine alert, a wake-up call meant to make you the person God has called you to be. Then, like Peter, respond appropriately.

Lord, thank you for disturbing my peace when I grieve you.
Help me to respond appropriately.

1) John 13:38

2) Luke 22:62

3) Matthew 4:18-20

4) John 21:15-19

5) Psalm 23:3a

"For we know that if our earthly house, this tent,
is destroyed, we have a building from God,
a house not made with hands, eternal in the heavens."

One day a man of modest means, living in a tent, begins thinking he ought to upgrade to a more permanent place. His present arrangement is alright for the moment. The tent has been a very good one, but its maintenance has worn him down as life's storms have so weathered it's fabric. It seems to him that any day the whole place could come apart - then where would he be? Wisely, when a generous, non-retractable offer comes to his attention he decides to explore it. It is from the tent's manufacturer. As things would have it, they also build houses. This builder says, if the tent owner will agree to his contract (and he gives him a copy of it to read), he will guarantee him a house. In fact, he says, he will personally see that the house is ready in time for the tent's inevitable failure. As an incentive for the tent owner to take the deal, the manufacturer even goes so far as to promise he will both meet the present tent's maintenance needs now *and* throw in a lot of gratuities with the new house later. All of this gained the tent owner's attention, but the whole thing sounds too good to be true. Not to be taken in, he opens the builder's contract and checks out the details. Everything seems in order. He even learns the new house has already been paid for at the builder's expense![1] Overwhelmed and teary-eyed, knowing he is about to receive something he could never obtain on his own, the tent owner reaches out a trembling hand. When he does, the builder grasps it and pulls the tent owner close to Him for a warm embrace.[2]

Lord, thank you for the future, permanent,

perfect body I look forward to receiving from you.

1 Peter 1:18-19

2) Malachi 3:17

"Today, if you will hear His voice..."

In 1963, I was a high school student sitting in an eighth grade music class listening to an opera. Suddenly, a large wall speaker crackled on. It was the principle, and his voice called everyone to listen attentively to an important announcement. With recognizable sadness he informed us our then United States President, John F. Kennedy, had been assassinated. Upon hearing this, students turned towards each other with bewildered looks... immediately released from school, we returned to our homes anxious to hear more of what had happened, to ponder upon what it all meant.

In 2001, when what came to be called 9-11 occurred, I was working alone in the back of a large auto parts warehouse. Quietly stocking shelves, I had my thoughts to myself when my boss happened by to retrieve a part. "Hey," he said with a little alarm, "something is happening at the World Trade Center in New York." "What's that," I asked. "Something about a plane hitting one of the towers." "Huh?" I said. "What kind of plane?" "I don't know, just caught the end of a radio report. I'm sure we'll hear more." And hear more we did, all so disturbing and difficult as it was.

At a time between the two aforementioned events, another world shaking thing happened. A young lady and I were sitting, eating ice cream cones in the front bucket seats of my 1978 Mustang. While enjoying our treat, she shared with me how Jesus had died for my sins and risen from the dead. Not unlike the events previously mentioned, hearing of this left me dumbfounded, my mind stretched to take it in, and I hungered for more information. Eventually, I came to believe

Jesus died as the substitute for my sin and my life was never the same.

There are world shaking events in every generation, and awareness of each will not be in everyone's personal experience. However, knowledge of, and information about Christ's life and sacrifice is the one necessary world shaking event this and every forthcoming generation needs to hear. The spiritual nature of what Christ accomplished makes Him the only way by which people can receive eternal life.[1] Hearing and responding to that reality is what can bring any person[2] into a personal relationship with the living God. This is why no other world shaking events have had, or will ever have, so profound an impact as what God accomplished through His son.[3] It's the one world shaker people really do need to hear about.[4]

Lord, you have my attention. Help me learn all I can about you and your wonderful son.

1) John 14:6

2) John 6:37

3) Acts 4:12

4) John 4:35; Romans 10:13,14

"Fight the good fight of faith, lay hold on eternal life..."

An oft referred to "fog of war" engulfed the marines of First Battalion, Fifth Division. It happened when they were headed into Bagdad to take over Saddam Hussein's royal palace. The problem began after part of the convoy took a wrong turn. This caused vehicles to become separated and travel down wrong roads in the city. Suddenly, using rocket propelled grenades, mortars and machine gun fire, Iraqi forces initiated a heavy attack on the convoy. Any previous quiet was immediately replaced by the noise of battle. Logistical coordination to get back on track became hampered by communication problems. The result was confusion... "the fog of war" set in on the American soldiers. Moving forward out of harm's way took on even greater urgency, but the situation had become a worse-case scenario... the separated convoy had entirely lost its way. Through it all, despite the difficulties the vehicles kept moving. While they did, soldiers remained active in figuring out what path to take, they did not stop. In a predicament like this, that is the protocol the soldiers are trained to follow... to keep moving. This is because experience has proven, it is harder for the enemy to hit a moving target. So, as they moved, they worked out getting their directions straight, eventually finding the correct way and moving in the right direction. Soon they reached the palace and overwhelmed its defenders. This was not an easy day, but it certainly was one to be remembered.

Followers of Jesus have times in their lives like that, when they are enveloped by something similar to the "fog of war." It happens when the enemy throws everything he has at them and the result is their communication with others, maybe even with God, becomes strained and confusion sets in. They are tempted to arrive at a standstill, to stop going to church, stop praying, stop seeking fellowship with God's people. This temptation to stop moving forward, to come to a standstill rather than press toward a previously planned goal and victory, puts a Christian in great danger. What should be done? Why, of course, they should not stop, they should - keep moving.

What should you do when under attack? Do not stop moving toward your goal, toward the victory God has for you - keep moving! When the enemy is doing his dirty work, desirous to defeat your advance and bring you to a stop - keep moving! Keep your eye on the Way (Jesus) and the way will open up before you.[1] Fight the good fight and keep moving![2] Victory is ahead.[3]

Lord, help me be consistent in my spiritual advance...

help me to keep moving.

1) 1 Corinthians 15:57

2) 1 John 5:4

3) Philippians 3:13, 14

"...put on tender mercies, kindness, humility, meekness, long-suffering; bearing with one another, and forgiving one another..."

I did something the other day I should not have done. Without sensitivity and moving too fast I "cut in line" ahead of another person. We'd both been waiting to speak with the same individual and, when I saw the opportunity, I took it. When this happened what actually took place was up for debate, or so I thought. You see, there was no "line" of people into the person's office. "Well," you may say," Then you did not cut in line." You might be right about that, and it is at first how I felt about this, but the man who I passed going into that office, the one who would take offense of me, he certainly saw it another way and he told me so.

The first moments of a relational confrontation are always immensely important. It is there an early opportunity exists to quell what may otherwise escalate in difficulty. The Scriptures offer the best course of action. It is to use a soft answer to turn away wrath.[1] I have at times utilized this wisdom and it works, but I failed to do so in this instance. Instead, I took a defensive attitude, seeking to justify and explain from my perspective what had happened. Not good. I'd forgotten, the best defense is often not a self-defense. Better to humble oneself,[2] to apologize for real or perceived wrong doing. I've no doubt, had I done that, the rift between myself and the other man would have been avoided. Due to my pride, it wasn't.

Later the same day our paths crossed again. Though we briefly spoke together of our earlier encounter, there was no consensus between us as to what had actually occurred. That might have been the end of the matter (and the end of any possibility of any fully restored relationship), except that God worked on me overnight and helped me to see things from His perspective. Sufficiently humbled, the next day I was prayed up and anxious to apologize.

My chance to eat "humble pie" came sooner than I had expected. Surprisingly, my counterpart turned out to be the first person I ran into the next day. How would he respond to my apology? He might sniff at it or, worse yet, reject it altogether and berate me on my slowness to do the right thing. When you get down to it, there is no guarantee on how such a communication will be received. Nonetheless, as I approached him I said, "Friend, I was wrong and stubborn yesterday, I apologize for it and hope you will forgive me." This is how he blessed me in response... he held out his hand, I took it and we shook hands. He said nothing. He didn't have to. The handshake said everything that needed to be said between us. What's more, I feel that handshake says the rest on this subject I would otherwise think I needed to say to you.

Lord, make me a humble person who can apologize quickly,

also help me to quickly accept the apology of others.

1) Proverbs 15:1

2) Proverbs 6:3

"Show me your ways, O LORD; teach me Your paths."

In my day, when as children we were asked what we enjoyed most about our primary school education, we would gleefully reply, "Show and Tell!" Recess came next as a close second choice.

What put Show and Tell at the top of our interest list? Weren't subjects like reading, writing and arithmetic enough to excite us? No, not like Show and Tell. I mean, let's face it, what could be more jaw dropping than Suzy showing and telling about her Betsy Wetsy, a doll that could actually wet itself like a real baby! Then there was Jimmy with his Mattel Tiger Tank, a battery operated toy that moved and delivered explosive blows with its working cannon! How about Andy holding up a new Mickey Mantle baseball card he was pleased to find in a package of Topps bubble gum! (Did I just date myself?) You must admit, that's a hard to beat line-up that would have to get and excite any child's attention!

God knows the powerful attraction of Show and Tell. That is why He has His own impossible to beat line-up of things to excite us. He shows off the stars of heaven, then tells us, "These declare my glory!"[1] He reveals to us the varied geography of the earth's surface and declares, "This firmament shows my handiwork!"[2] He points to people and says, "I've made them in my image!"[3] He permits us a view of the oceans and proclaims, "One day the knowledge of me will cover the earth like the vastness of these seas."[4]

While God loves to show and tell about many things, among them the wonders of nature, there is only one that is His favorite, His first choice. Next to this, everything else takes second place. This is because His first choice is the focal point, the reason, for all other things.[5] What is God's first choice for Show and Tell? None other than His own son, Jesus Christ.[6]

God shows His son in a manger and tells us, "This is the Savior I promised."[7] He shows His son living a sinless life and says, "This is my one mediator between me and man."[8] He shows His son can forgive sin and proclaims, "I have given Him all authority in Heaven and on earth."[9] He shows a cross with His son hanging on it and declares, "I give Him as a sacrifice to redeem people who will believe on Him."[10]

There is no way around it, Show and Tell is never more jaw dropping than when God does the showing and telling!

Lord, thank you for showing me your son and telling me about Him.

1) Psalm 19:1a

2) Psalm 19:1b

3) Genesis 1:27

4) Isaiah 11:9

5) Colossians 1:17

6) Luke 9:35

7) Isaiah 7:14

8) 1 Timothy 2:5

9) Matthew 28:1

10) John 3:16

"Seek the LORD while He may be found,
call upon Him while He is near."

Going astray is no joking matter! To depart from a place of belonging is to enter endangered territory.

One day, a friend dropped by with a horse and invited my young daughter to ride it. Not all that experienced with horses, we boosted her up one side of the animal, only to have her slide off onto the ground on its other side. I suppose the horse was unaccustomed to such a thing, because he promptly took off riderless for parts unknown. He was astray! What to do? A riderless horse in an urban area was certainly in danger as well as a hazard to others. The horse's owner and I took off in my car and hailed people along the streets. Our stock question was (you could probably guess it), "Which way did he go?" The directions we received led us between houses and down roadways until we finally spotted the panting horse. He was standing in front of a business establishment where he had been reined in by an alert cowboy. That horse's going astray certainly gave both him and a lot of other people some very anxious moments!

Another animal's decision to "fly the coup" led to more serious consequence than did the horse. This time it was a dog. I brought him home and he made a big hit with the family. That is, until the day he got hit. Finding a door ajar, the normally inside pet promptly went astray. A short time after, I found him dead in the roadway in front of our house. He'd had the misfortune of running into something he'd never have encountered had he stayed under his owner's protection.

The possibility of going astray and the negative consequences of doing so is not limited to animals. Isaiah 53:6 says, "All we like sheep have gone astray; we have turned, every one, to his own way." It is no accident that the Holy Spirit inspired Scriptures often equate people to sheep.[1] By nature sheep are prone to stray, so are people. Therein lies the importance of staying under the care of the Good Shepherd who has our best interests at heart.[2] Such a one is Jesus, the Shepherd and Bishop (Caretaker) of our souls.[3] We are safest when we can admit we are prone to wander and committed enough to remain by our Shepherd's side.[4] We don't belong astray.[5] Apart from our Shepherd we find ourselves in endangered territory, with need of "reigning in" before we take the "big hit" that can cost us dearly.[6]

If you are astray from God in any way today, admit it and make tracks to remedy your situation by drawing close to Him.[7] You will find in Him a place of belonging and safety when you do.[8]

Lord, I admit I am prone to wander. Help me learn the wisdom of

staying close to you.

1) Psalm 100:3; 119:176   5) Psalm 61:1-4

2) John 10:11   6) Proverbs 14:12

3) 1 Peter 2:25   7) James 4:8; John 6:37

4) Psalm 143:9, 10   8) Matthew 11:28-30; Psalm 4:8

"But who do you say that I am?"

It's been awhile, but I haven't forgotten what fun a game could be with a gathering of friends. One game I remember was called, "Who Am I?" To play it a host would pin the name of a famous person on each participant's back. Unable to see it, no one knew what name they had received. Therein was the challenge - people would walk around asking one another questions in an effort to determine who they were. The first person to correctly figure out their new identity was the winner!

Responses to Jesus' question, "Who am I?" were at first interesting but inaccurate. He was not John the Baptist, not Elijah or one of the prophets as people thought.[1] Sometimes questions need to be repeated before correct answers are attained, such was true here. So Jesus asked again, "Who do you say I am?" This time Peter responded accurately when he responded, "You are the Christ."[2] Bingo! We have a winner! Identity discovered! Jesus is the Christ.

Jesus asks the same question of you, He asks, "Who am I?" Teachers do not accept incomplete answers on tests and neither does Jesus. If you respond that He is an exceptional man, or a good example to follow, it is not enough. Remember Peter's response? He said, "You are the Christ." This was an acceptable, complete answer. Peter's use of the title "Christ" (it is not Jesus' last name) conveyed his belief that Jesus was the Anointed One of God, the promised Messiah, the Savior of the world! This is the answer you want to arrive at to have confidence of eternal life and your entrance through heaven's gate.[3]

Once you answer the identity of Jesus correctly there is a "game change." The question you will then ask others is, "Who is He?" This encourages them to discover the answer to life's most necessary question. Getting this right is of eternal importance. A person's present and future well-being depends on if they can deliver an accurate answer.[4] Hopefully you will have opportunity to repeat for them the necessary question, "Who is He?" until such time as their answer is complete.[5]

Lord Jesus, I believe you are the Christ. Help me to help others discover this truth.

1) Mark 8:28

2) Mark 8:29b

3) John 20:31

4) Hebrews 9:27

5) Proverbs 30:4

"If you do not do well, sin lies at the door."

Sin is undesirable because it is a persistent antagonist to the human soul. Like dew on grass in early morning, sin often seems to appear out of nowhere.

Our family once had a pet peacock and its one redeeming quality was its beauty. Aside from that, it made aggravating noises and left piles of manure anywhere and everywhere, sometimes right at the foot of our front door! Often we would be eating at the dining table inside the house while the peacock stood outside staring at us through the screen door.

Sin is like that: always staring at us, looking for an opportunity to gain entrance to our lives. It is deceptively attractive and always ready to make obnoxious noises in our soul. The best thing to do is to keep sin at a distance and not get too close, otherwise we can get into a real mess.

One day I decided it was time to disable the peacock's ability to fly, something that requires pulling a few of its flight feathers. First, I chased the bird down. Second, I tucked the creature backward under my right arm. Third, the bird promptly let loose with one of its warm messes all over my bare foot! My observing children thought this was hilarious... I on the other hand, was less impressed.

Tackling sin should be left to an expert. If we try to do it ourselves, without an expert's assistance, we will be put in a mess. Thank God, though sin would like to overcome us, there is one who can conquer it for us.[1]

When we are aware sin is at the door, let's ask Jesus to handle it.

Lord, when I sense sin's approach remind me

not to try to tackle it by myself.

1) Romans 8:37

"For when I am weak, then I am strong."

I realized something today. It came along with hearing a powerful testimony by a very weak man. Here is his story...

As a young man he served as a dog handler during the Vietnam War. One day, when moving as point man for his squad, both he and his dog took the first shots fired during an ambush by the Vietcong. The dog was killed, but the man survived – barely. They had actually tagged him dead before an alert orderly became aware he had a very weak pulse. He was kept alive on the battlefield and, after one month comatose, he awakened in a hospital. Every form of speech therapy was given to him, the result being that he gained back speech. He also regained some movement of his right arm, but ever since this he has been in a wheelchair with little else physically going for him. Yet what spiritual victory he has! Sitting next to his wife of 37 years, he gave all glory to God for his life. We too, listening to him, sometimes laughing, sometimes crying, also had to give God glory.

So, what was it I realized as a result of this man's testimony? It is this... that after 41 years of my being a believer, I know the most powerful testimonies I have heard come from people like this man, believers who are among the world's most physically weak individuals. In many cases, they do not have the capacity to lift a drinking cup to their lips, yet they give evidence of an inner peace, an amazing sense of humor and a positive outlook on life. Should these peoples' lives not speak loudly to we who have physical strength, the full use of our appendages, and freedom to move our bodies around at will whenever we want? Shouldn't observing the victorious living of these people, maybe, just maybe awaken us to wanting what they have? I do not mean we should want or ask God for their physical circumstance. But ought we not, in the midst of whatever problems and challenges we face, be able to give evidence in our own lives of having the same inner peace, humor and positive outlook that these people demonstrate? I think we should. After all, when it comes to being weak spiritually, we are all equally weak. Initially each of us is dead in our sins and in need of being made alive in Christ. Dead is weaker than weak, isn't it? Dead is, well, you know – dead! Fortunately though, after we receive Christ as our Savior, in the strength of the new life He gives us we can lift a spiritual cup of water to our lips and drink. This is what many physically weak individuals with powerful testimonies all have in common... they consistently drink of the waters that never run dry.[1] They drink continually and deeply from God's Word. We who are physically strong can do this too. This is the way that, as with our physically weaker brothers and sisters, Christ will become our strength.[2] We ought to realize our need and, doing something about it – we should drink.

Lord, help me realize just how weak I am without you. I want to drink of your life giving water.

1) John 4:14

2) Philippians 4:13

"We who live are always delivered to death for Jesus' sake..."

I once had a dog named Jack. All was fine with him until, one day, out of the blue, he decided to jump out the window of a moving vehicle I was driving. In my side view mirror I saw him hit the pavement, legs all splayed out, his head on one side hitting the ground hard. "Oh Jack, you stupid dog, why did you go and do that?" I said it even as all at the same time I stopped, pulled on the emergency brake, and leapt out of the van. So far as I could see, though stunned, he was not horribly banged up. For the most part it appeared he did recover. It was the other part that bothered me. After that incident he seemed to be more aggressive towards strangers, less the dog to be comfortable around. Eventually my discomfort about what he might be capable of reached a crisis point and I decided for safety reasons Jack might need to be "put down."

On my way to make arrangements for the deed to be done, I experienced a great deal of inner turmoil about the decision I was making. After all, Jack got along wonderfully with me – it was his getting along well with others that bothered me. Yet, to be honest, to my knowledge nothing bad had actually happened. This made me wonder, was I really justified to terminate Jack's life? But, oh well, the deed was done and Jack was then a couple of feet under, buried in my own back yard. I, it seemed, would be forever left to question if I had done the right thing... then there was an unanticipated development.

The same day Jack was dispatched and buried there was a knock at the door. When I answered it I found a man and a boy standing outside, both with sad faces. I noticed too, one of the boy's arms was bandaged. "I've come to inform you," the father said, "that earlier today your dog came out from under your fence, bit my son on his arm, then retreated back into your yard." When I heard this my jaw dropped. I felt so bad. I was thinking I ought to have put Jack down sooner – before this boy got hurt! I apologized profusely to them both and offered to pay the medical expense. Then I did something that made me feel good, real good. I walked both of them over to the disturbed soil that had been a freshly dug hole in my yard, pointed to it and said to the boy, "That dog that bit you this morning is here, dead and buried. He will never, never threaten you or anyone else again!"

Had I been justified to put Jack down? The same day visit by that father and son say I was. Similarly, is it possible there is something in your life that, for your own and others safety, you need to bury before someone gets hurt?[1] I encourage you, if you've a nagging discomfort that you may be harboring something detrimental in your life, deal with it before it gets out and bites someone.[2]

Lord, help me to not harbor anything in my life that could be detrimental to myself or others.

1) Galatians 5:15

2) Romans 6:11-13

"As the Father has sent Me, I also send you."

Years ago there was a popular B & W television show entitled, "Have Gun Will Travel." It was set in the early West and had a main character whose name was Paladin. He sported fancy clothes, good manners and a gun. Using a business card embossed with the show title and a chess piece logo, Paladin advertised he was available to go where he was needed to help beleaguered people oppose obnoxious enemies.

Obedient Christians are a lot like Paladin. They make themselves available to go where they are needed. Most of the time, this just means their being available to family or a near neighbor, but sometimes it can mean even going so far as the ends of the earth.[1]

Like Paladin, Christ followers are also ready to help people stand up to their enemies, the enemies of their souls – the world, the flesh and the devil. Their weapon of choice, unlike Paladin's, is a sword, "the Word of God that is living, powerful and sharp."[2] With this sword they "subdue kingdoms, work righteousness and obtain God's promises."[3]

Paladin was a well-dressed man: so are the Lord's messengers. God has clothed them in "fine linen, clean and bright.[4] This is Christ's righteousness which has replaced the old clothes they had inherited from Adam. What's more, their good manners, demonstrated in their walking with the Lord, compliment their apparel.[5]

I ask you – are you ready to go where you are needed? Are you properly dressed, equipped, mannered and motivated to be a spiritual Paladin? Can you use the two-edged sword, the Word of God, to deliver beleaguered people from their soul's enemy, the devil? If you are, then you are God's Paladin and you can say, "Have Sword Will Travel."

Lord, I want the training and discipline needed to
be a ready and willing messenger for you.

1) Acts 1:8

2) Hebrews 4:12

3) Hebrews 11:33

4) Revelation 19:8

5) Ephesians 4:1-3

"Beloved, do not think it strange

concerning the fiery trial which is to try you..."

Do you enjoy taking tests? A lot of people do not. I can't say as I do. Tests have a way of making us feel uneasy, threatened, and anxious. After all, with testing comes the possibility of failure, of falling short of passing. So I get it, I can identify with the discomfort associated with testing. If I could choose the testing format, that would help. In school I would always prefer multiple choice questions. Actually, we called them, "multiple guess tests" because you always had the chance of guessing the right answer if you were not sure. The next best choice for me was the fill in the blanks kind of test. The very last thing I wanted to see was the dreaded essay question that would need completing! Curiously, I don't remember any teacher ever asking what testing format I would prefer. They just did what they were going to do for reasons best known to them - no explanation given.

Thinking about this reminds me of how the Lord tests His children. They do not get to choose the format of the test, the "fiery trial" allowed to challenge them in order to prove and deepen their faith. The Lord has many formats to choose from, and He is under no obligation to explain why He chooses one over another as He assigns them among us. For one person it is illness, another a prison stay, others persecution, financial woes or a loved one's seemingly untimely death. His list of possible kinds of tests is long.

Do believers know when they are being tested? Sure. When tested they feel uneasy, anxious, perhaps even threatened by their circumstance. After all, the trial, the situation God has allowed them to get into, is a challenge to their faith. Admittedly, theirs is not a written test measurable on paper, like a test of their Bible knowledge might be. No, theirs is a life test which measures their faith. It is a test custom designed in God's infinite wisdom to prove, strengthen and increase their faith and bring Him glory. What's more, God's testing enhances His child's "test–imony," their personal experience of the reality of God's grace and power to bring them through tough times. This makes faith attractive to other people who not only need to hear the good news, but who also need to see how this good news can be victoriously lived out in the nitty-gritty challenges of life.

No question about it, God's testing can be tough, but it has as it's purpose only what is good for His children.[1] With this in mind, I suggest that you be courageous,[2] and face what comes your way with confidence no matter what mode of testing the Lord employs for you.

Lord, I trust you. Help me to have a positive attitude
about life and its challenges.

1) Romans 8:28

2) Ephesians 6:10

"Faith is the substance of things hoped for,
the evidence of things not seen."

Some people see things that just aren't there. Recently I spent time with a man who was seeing a dog and people. The only problem was – they weren't there! He would speak and interact with them, but they weren't there! To make matters worse, they would not do what he wanted. The dog wouldn't get out of his way and the people would not assist in getting him out of his room or bringing him what he demanded. Suffice it to say, he was an agitated, aggravated man, challenging to be around. That is because, for others, seeing things clearly did not include seeing what he saw, things that just weren't there. Seeing things as he was is not a good way to relate to reality, to what really is. It is easy to imagine how viewing things that way would lead to frustration.

Each of us needs to perceive things as they really are or we will fall to frustration. This is an important concept for those who would seek to follow Christ. By faith, followers of Christ can see a great many things invisible to the naked eye, things that inform their beliefs and actions. The difference between these things and those the gentleman I described saw is that the things believers see are really present. They conform to reality, to what really is. For instance, we see Jesus[1] and, in seeing Him, we see God.[2] We also see God's invisible attributes,[3] and some of us have seen angels.[4] Such things conform to reality so, contrary to being frustrated, we are blessed, peaceful and satisfied. What's more, we are inheritors of eternal life![5]

If you are "seeing things" with the eyes of faith that conform to the Word of God – don't stop! However, if you are seeing God or the world you live in inaccurately, it is best to ask God for help. You will save yourself and others a lot of frustration if you do. Go ahead, call on Him. You have an open invitation from Him to do so. He says, "Call to me, and I will answer you."[6]

Lord, help me to see my world through your eyes.

I want to see it as it really is.

1) Hebrews 12:2

2) John 12:45

3) Romans 1:20

4) Hebrews 13:2

5) 1 Peter 1:3-5

6) Jeremiah 33:3

"...be vigilant..."

At one time, while living in West Africa, I had a management responsibility for a compound guard named Saidu. He was a friendly young man who, when his duties allowed it, would weave decorative ground mats while on the job. That was not a problem, but his sleeping during his turn for night duty was. The first time I became aware of it he and I discussed the matter. He agreed his work of guarding the compound's people and facilities required alertness. After all, reports of night guards injured or killed were not uncommon. Although we had that talk, one night soon after it I got up from my own sleep to go out and check on him. There he was soundly asleep on his ground mat. What to do? To impress the seriousness of this behavior upon him I left him sleeping, but carried off his bow and arrows. Imagine his chagrin when he woke up at some point and discovered his defenses had been down!

Being "caught with your pants down" is a proverbial saying most people understand. Saidu would have known this and certainly King Saul too. Nonetheless, one time Saul went into a cave to relieve himself. Unaware he was not alone, David was able to slice off a piece of Saul's clothing. That fragment of cloth became evidence to the embarrassing fact that, for lack of vigilance, Saul had made himself vulnerable to harm.[1] On another occasion a similar thing happened. While Saul slept, David stole away with his spear and drinking jug.[2] It seems King Saul and Saidu had something in common - not a good thing... neither appears to have learned his need to be alert and aware to danger.[3]

How about you? Have you learned to be alert to your own welfare? If you are a follower of Christ, you must learn this or put yourself in danger from your adversary, the devil. Your defenses are down if you are not praying, not daily in God's Word, not witnessing for Christ and not serving others with what God has gifted you to do. If you measure yourself by such imperatives as these, how alert are you?[4]

Lord, strengthen me to keep my personal defenses

in place against the devil's schemes.

1) 1 Samuel 24:3-11

2) 1 Samuel 26:7-12

3) 1 Thessalonians 5:6

4) 1 Peter 5:8

"...He saw also a certain poor widow putting in two mites."

I enjoyed making handcrafts as a child. I made them at school, church, scout meetings, summer camps and home. The endless variety of things that could be put together with white glue, paper mache, colored paper, sequins, egg cartons, beads, boxes and cans were, I think, all made by me at one time or another. There was one project among the many I made that especially stands out in my mind. I put a lot of effort into it. It was a pen and pencil holder which I made to give my dad one Father's Day. Here is how I did it... first, I attached colored paper around the surface of an empty vegetable can. Second, I used white glue to stick on a mixture of sequins and glitter. Next, I used a crayon and wrote, "DAD," in a space I had left open. When I looked at it, I thought it was the greatest thing I had ever made. Nonetheless, I was nervous about how my gift might be received. This was because I knew my father could purchase any professionally manufactured pen and pencil holder he wanted.

When Father's day arrived and my project was unwrapped, my father appeared thrilled, genuinely appreciative of my gift. As a matter of fact, for years afterward that pen and pencil holder had a special place at his desk. Strange though, for over the same course of years, the way I viewed things changed. I came to no longer see the pen and pencil holder, or my father, as I had in the past. I had grown to understand that my father received and used the holder, not because of how great it was, or even that he needed it, but he delighted and used it because of how much he loved me and appreciated my effort to please him.

The way my earthly father received and made use of that holder is similar to how our heavenly Father responds when we bring our gifts to Him. Consider all the wonderful things He already possesses... the heavens, the earth and all that is in them for a start.[1] This makes whatever we give Him at best only a humble offering. Even though this is the case, He is pleased to receive and use the gifts we bring to Him.[2]

Big or small, much or little, all our gifts are humble gifts in light of what our heavenly Father already owns and enjoys.[3] What He looks for from us are gifts given in love – whatever those gifts may be.

Lord, because you are worthy, help me to give in the way
that brings you the greatest pleasure.

1) Psalm 89:11

2) Malachi 3:10

3) Psalm 113:4-6

"Behold, I stand at the door and knock..."

Arriving at the door of a home to which I had previously received casual invitation I knocked, then waited to see if I'd be welcomed inside. To my delight, a young lady of former acquaintance swung open the door and asked me in. Things were awkward for her at first. We didn't know each other very well, but as we engaged in conversation she started to relax. After a while it appeared I had won her trust. That was when she asked me, the interior designer, to inspect her house and give her my considerably expert advice as to what could be done to update her living quarters. Her intent was to make her place more attractive and comfortable to live in. We were sitting in her living room so, after we signed a written agreement, it was natural I begin my observations there. The living room was definitely in need of attention. Books, not all of wholesome content, were strewn about, and pictures on the walls were not in keeping with the brilliant living colors I would like to have seen. Worst of all (and I soon discovered this was true for all the rooms) the home's lighting was dismal. It was difficult to understand how, if at all, this woman was able to get around without banging herself up. Taking a deep breath, I calmly offered her my best advice. "Things need be put in order if you are going to fully enjoy this place. Some of these books need to be discarded, others ought to be returned to the shelf, and new materials need to be acquired and put prominently on display." Gauging her reaction to what I said, I looked carefully at her. We seemed to be off to an agreeable start. She was nodding her head. I was encouraged, so I kept on going. "Also," I said, "the pictures on your walls - their subject matter is not at all in keeping with the new atmosphere we want to create. They should be replaced with subjects in living colors. What would you say to things like an ocean scene, children playing, flowers, subjects of that nature?" Again, her response was very positive. "I think I'd like that very much," she said. "Wonderful," I responded. "The one other thing requiring immediate attention is the lighting in here – it's too dark." "Really?" she offered, "I hadn't noticed, but now that you're here, I think I do see what you're saying." "Actually," she continued, "The lighting is like this in all my rooms." Yes, I said, "I noticed. I'm going to suggest installation of new, high energy lighting in every room, darkness is contrary to what we want to accomplish here." "I see," she replied. "Well then, more light is in order. I think I am beginning to understand where you are going with this." "Where I am going with your permission," I said, "is into that closet over there." "No, please, not there!" "Oh," I replied, "Did I misunderstand what you wanted? Wasn't I to join you in your home's renewal?" "Well, yes, but must we go into the closet?" "It is part of your home, is it not?" I asked. "Yes, of course it is, it's just that, well, the contents of that closet are especially embarrassing to me." "I see. I think I detect some shame. It's all the more reason to clean the closet out. What would you say to our doing it together? I'm especially good about such things." "When you put it like that," she said, "how could I refuse." "That's the Spirit!" I replied, and we did it together, we cleaned the closet out. It was hard – not for me, but for her. I helped her get through it though, and she was so grateful! We definitely grew closer doing it together.

Today, my friend's home is a real showcase, a far healthier, enjoyable place for us to spend time. Oh, did I forget to mention it? She appreciated what I've done for her so much - she invited me to stay! It's a fact... now I am sticking to her closer than a brother.[1]

Lord, thank you for living in me.

Show me if there is anything I need to release to you.

1.) John 14:16, 17; Proverbs 18:24

"... like a rolling thing before the whirlwind."

Watch an authentic western movie and at some point you will certainly see tumbleweeds being blown around by the wind. The plant originated in Russia and somehow found its way over to the United States. First recognized in South Dakota in 1880, this Russian thimble was labeled under the scientific name "salsola tragus." A rapid reproducer, today it grows everywhere in the United States except Florida and Alaska. The plant can become quite a nuisance. It totally dries out each winter, becomes brittle, then breaks off at its base. From there the wind catches it and it starts to move. This is when it can become trouble as it creates a lot of extra work needing to be cleared away from stationary objects like buildings and fences where tumbleweeds tend to accumulate. This plant, which seems to have no apparent purpose, is aptly described by its detractors as "a very obnoxious weed."

In Isaiah 17:3-13 the prophet used more than a few images to describe the failure of Israel's people to follow God. One of those images used is the lowly tumbleweed. [Note: In Isaiah 17:13 NKJV "rolling thing" is the same as "tumbleweed" in Hebrew.] The tumbleweed offers a good illustration of a nation not rooted in God's will, on loose from God and, for lack of purpose, moved about in any direction the winds of time may blow.

What is said of a nation can be said of its people. Today the United States of America is spiritually dry, as brittle as a tumbleweed. Our culture has lost so much application of our past Christian heritage that, instead of being rooted in God and allowing for His guidance, our citizens blow wherever the wind takes them.   Like tumbleweeds, problems result because of it.

Some people escape being spiritual tumbleweeds, but how about you? If you have been tumbling about in life, stop where you are and become, "like a tree planted by the rivers of water, that brings forth its fruit in its season, whose leaf also shall not wither; and whatever he does shall prosper."[1]

Wherever you are is a good place to set down roots in God's Word, then you will be "steadfast and unmovable," well rooted, "always abounding in the work of the Lord."[2] In that condition, no one will ever be able to call you a "spiritual tumbleweed."

Lord, I want my faith and practice
to be firmly planted in you and your Word.

1) Psalm 1:3

2) 1 Corinthians 15:58

"The Lord will whistle for the fly... and bee... and they will come."

A well trained dog is something I am not very familiar with. We had a dog, but he was not well trained, or obedient. His name was Bucky. He and his dog house were passed on to our family after he was already big and full grown. He had a hefty bark and regularly scared people who approached him. After only a short time with us we began to question the wisdom of having taken responsibility for him. Then, one day, a cat in the neighborhood was chewed up by a dog. Someone suggested that Bucky did it, but no one was sure. To be on the safe side I secured him in the yard anyway. Not long afterward, I arrived home to find Bucky had gotten loose. To make matters worse, there he was in the front yard with a cat in his mouth! Unable to stop him, he violently shook the unfortunate animal to death right in front of me. The next day I took Bucky to the city pound where they promptly euthanized him.

The story of Bucky is not a happy one, but there are worse things that can happen. Sometimes it is people who behave badly and pay the price for it. No doubt the life of an animal does not measure up to the life of a person made in the image of God. That is not to say that the lives of both humans and the animals cannot be mourned. Everything has been made by God for His glory, so whenever things happen that do not reflect the way things ought to be it is sad. In this fallen world, if the Lord allows us the privilege of living a lifetime, we are sure to witness many sad matters.

To counter the discouragement and disillusionment of things not being the way they were meant to be, we need to be ardent appreciators of the sovereignty of God. It is accurate to say that God either directs something to happen, or He allows it to happen: either way, as we trust Him, faith in His sovereignty permits us to have confidence that "all things work together for good to those who love God, to those who are the called according to His purpose."[1] You may want to repeat that verse again and emphasize the word "all." It is a thoroughly inclusive word that leaves nothing out... even the cat killing dogs that must be euthanized or, of even greater consequence, whole armies of people God calls out to do His will in relation to the rise and fall of nations. The prophet Isaiah understood this truth and God used him to illustrate this fact.

Isaiah said God only had to whistle for the armies of Egypt (the fly) and Assyria (the bee) to obey Him. (I couldn't even get Bucky to do that!) [Note: the words "hiss for the fly" in Isaiah 7:18 KJV literally mean in Hebrew "to whistle" as used in the NKJV.] God used enemy armies to humble His people for their own good. By doing so He moved His people from trusting in false sources of earthly deliverance and turned them to Himself for their salvation. During perplexing times, Isaiah was kept from despair by his belief that God was in control of everything, that God had his and his nation's ultimate good in mind. He knew God's seemingly harsh action of having foreign armies attack his nation, would ultimately culminate in their own kingdom of peace and safety.[2]

Sad to say, but my kingdom of peace and safety only returned after Bucky was gone. Eventually we got another dog – one that would come when I whistled.

Lord, when bad things happen, help me remember that you are in control and you are good.

1.) Romans 8:28   2) Isaiah 9:2-7

"... not forsaking the assembling of ourselves together, as is the manner of some..."

People are a lot like turtles... they only make progress when they stick their necks out! Some, even many professing Christians, live in their homes and rarely "stick their necks out" to get where they need to go and grow spiritually. They may profess to know Christ, yet make little to no effort to assemble themselves together with other Christians. They get themselves out to go to movies, dine or shop, but not to go to church. At best, if genuine in their faith, such persons become like coals that, set apart from a hot fire, take on a cold status and are not able to warm the faith of others. People who are in this condition are often heard to say things like, "I can read my Bible at home" or, "I listen to a preacher on the radio or television." Some will even say, "I do not have to go to church to be a Christian." Such responses are largely without merit when held up against the light of Hebrews 10:25 which tells the faithful to not stop meeting together. The spiritual gifts that will mature a Christian's faith are the reason to not stop.[1] Only by "rubbing shoulders" with other people who have these gifts can a believer mature and benefit. Then, like a coal in a fire, they are able to keep others hot, fulfilling their purpose in a spiritually cold world.

Followers of Christ were meant to make an effort to come together. The Lord's own habit of faithfully meeting with others in the temple supports this.[2] Then, He met with God's people in the temple. Now, He joins in assembly wherever those He bought and paid for through His sacrifice meet.[3]

Just do it. Choose to please God by meeting regularly with others who pursue His Son. Like them, and like a turtle, to make progress you will have to stick your neck out of your house.

Lord, because you purchased your church by your sacrifice,

help me value your church enough to meet together with it.

1) 1 Corinthians 12:4-12

2) Matthew 26:55b

3) Acts 20:28; Matthew 18:20

"Please Him who enlisted you as a soldier."

The letters I.E.D. stand for "Improvised Explosive Device." These are weapons of war that afflicted heavy casualties among the American military in Afghanistan and Iraq wars. They are hidden explosives the enemy buries in roadways, otherwise hiding them where they can be remotely detonated, usually by cell phone. Sadly, early in these wars, I.E.D.s were lethal at injuring and killing many U.S. military personnel. When the devices went off beneath their vehicles, loss of limbs or death were all too common. Thankfully, after a time, alterations were made to their vehicles. To deflect a blast should one occur, angled, heavy metal plates were added to undercarriages in order to deflect an explosion's effectiveness. Thereafter, in the event a blast did happen, soldiers might still experience disorientation, hearing loss or injury, but death was less likely.

Satan has seen to it that this life is an I.E.D. minefield for Christians. He and his spiritual cohorts arrange that we have ample opportunity to run over traps they have prepared. They want to disable us and, if they can pull it off, kill us. Whichever the case, an explosion can leave us injured, with loss of hearing, even crippled spiritually and in need of healing. Fortunately, if we are Christ followers, we have been upgraded with deflector plates[1] and some of a blast's lethal impact will be directed away from us. As believers, we can be confident that the Lord has our backs.[2] He has the devil on a leash, so that destroyer cannot go farther than He permits.[3]

In the case of war, an Oklahoma City bombing, or Boston Marathon explosion, we see I.E.D.s that are of man's making. More often, enemy

I.E.D.s are spiritually laid in our own homes, at work or even in church. In the places we frequent, fractured communications, hurt feelings, lack of unity, or out of control anger are but a few of Satan's staging grounds where he hides life damaging devices.[4]

In life's battles we can take a lesson from our American brothers in arms. When traveling suspect paths where I.E.D.s are likely to be hidden, they look for anything that is out of place. It may be as simple as disturbed dirt which is a sign of possible I.E.D. burying. Or, it may be something out of order along the roadside. In either case, the possibility of danger is real. It must be addressed to insure safety. When an I.E.D. is found, it is disarmed, rendered inoperable, no longer dangerous. This is what we must do as good Christian soldiers... we must disarm the situations that may otherwise blow up in our faces. We do ourselves and others no favor if we disregard or turn a blind eye to disturbed dirt, to matters of danger to our Christian testimony, family or friends.

A good soldier has a strong sense of duty. He does due diligence to protect his own and other lives so they may live and fight another day. Let's be good soldiers for our Commander in Chief, the Lord Jesus Christ.[5] Let's be on the alert for spiritual I.E.D.s.

Lord, help me preserve myself and others from spiritual danger, guide my eyes and heart to recognize and disarm the traps of the devil.

1) Psalm 3:3a; 5:12   3) 1 Peter 3:22

2) Psalm 139:5   4) 2 Corinthians 2:11b   5) 2 Timothy 2:3,4

"For He made Him sin who knew no sin to be sin for us..."

The story is told of two brothers. They are close, but very different in their orientation towards life. The elder brother is a very responsible, dependable, trustworthy fellow. The younger is impetuous, foolish and always getting into trouble. The elder loves the younger, prays for him, and often appeals to him to change his ways.

One day the elder brother was startled when his workshop door abruptly opened. His brother crashed in with fear in his face, his shirt soaked with blood. Between gasps of breath he declared the police were fast approaching, he'd been in a fight and killed a man. Without hesitation, his elder brother commanded him to remove his shirt and exchange it with his own, then he pointed to the side door through which the younger brother quickly exited. When he did, the police entered the other door with their guns drawn. "There he is!" one declared, then another commanded the accused down on the ground, cuffed him and led him away.

While the younger brother kept a low profile, the older sibling was left to take the rap for him. That bloodied shirt, the one found on his elder brother at the time of his arrest, was believed by many to be the evidence that led to a successful death penalty conviction. It wasn't until after the execution that intense remorse about what happened overwhelmed the younger brother. Not knowing what else he could do to appease it, he sought an audience with the trial judge. Weeping, he laid out his story before him, and in conclusion said, "Your Honor, I confess it is I who killed that man. Do with me now what seems right to you." Laying his glasses aside, the judge looked into the face of the penitent and said, "Another has died in your place. He loved you enough to take the punishment you deserved. The court recognizes that love and his sacrifice. You are free to pursue living as you choose. I hope you choose wisely - it is the only way you have of honoring your brother's life and sacrifice... you are free to go."

Like that younger brother, because of your elder brother's sacrifice,[1] you too are free to go.[2] Choose wisely how you will live.[3]

Lord, thank you for taking my sin upon Yourself.
Help me honor you by the way I live.

1) Romans 8:29b

2) John 8:26

3) Joel 3:14

<u>Godchasers</u>

"Seek the Lord while He may be found..."

They are called "Stormchasers"... people who routinely make the effort to go where they can witness extreme weather, usually tornadoes. "Why would anyone want to do that?" If you ask that question, you are probably not a Stormchaser. For these people chasing storms is a passion, an intense desire that moves them to make an effort to experience something awesome and powerful. For those who are scientists, they do it to figure out how storms work. They want to dispel some of nature's mystery in hope of providing better weather forecasts and earlier warning systems that could save lives and property.

In the old days, before computers and cell phones, Stormchasers relied solely on paper maps and phone booths for weather updates. Today they have GPS, radar and electronic probes to assist them in their pursuit. Their search for extreme storms often takes them to a mid-western region of the United States referred to as "Tornado Alley." Although tornadoes have presented themselves in every state, big ones happen more there than anywhere else, so that is where Stormchasers focus their efforts.

An upsurge of people being interested in storm chasing followed the Hollywood blockbuster movie, "Twister." The Discovery television channel then sought to capitalize on this uptick of interest by launching a reality series called "Stormchasers." All this attention created such a mass of enthusiasts that now there is a concern for safety when their vehicles block escape routes leading away from approaching storms. Truth be told, participation in storm chasing carries with it an inescapable element of risk.

Three well known scientists were caught in a monstrous tornado and killed as recently as May 23, 2013. Storm chasing is definitely not for the faint of heart.

Similar to "Stormchasers," are "Godchasers"... people who routinely make the effort to get close to God.[1] You are probably not a Godchaser if you have to ask, "Why would anyone want to do that?"

These are people whose passionate desire to know God[2] moves them to get closer to Him.[3] They are Christ followers[4] who trust in a resurrected Savior and believe their sins are forgiven.[5] These people study the Bible and pray in expectation of increasing their experience with God.[6] What's more, they want to know His power so they may better warn others of impending danger.[7]

In the old days, before Christian films and DVDs, Godchasers used Old and then New Testaments as they became available. Today, they have complete Bibles in different translations, handheld electronic libraries, Christian television and radio programs, along with so much more that can assist them in their pursuit of God. Despite this proliferation of helps, their main source to confirm truth remains, as always and forever, the Word of God.[8] This speaks well for one region in the United States which compares favorably to the Stormchaser's Tornado Alley. It is a southern geographic area of the United States referred to as, "The Bible Belt."

An upsurge of involvement in God chasing was follow-up to a Hollywood blockbuster movie, "The Passion." Because of the film's portrayal, many people were motivated to consider the reality of Christ's suffering and sacrifice. This resulted in a renewed vision among believers, an increased willingness to make themselves available to lead others to safety. Like storm chasing, God chasing is not for the faint of heart.   One victim of the Columbine school shooting in Colorado, a fourteen year old girl, responded to her killer's question in the affirmative when he asked her, "Do you believe in God?" After she answered, "Yes," the young man promptly shot and killed her.

No question about it... like storm chasing, God chasing is not for the faint of heart.[9]

Lord, make me passionate in my quest to get closer to you.

1) Psalm 42:1,2a

2) Philippians 3:10

3) James 4:8

4) Matthew 4:19

5) Ephesians 1:7

6) 2 Timothy 2:15

7) Acts 1:8; John 3:18

8) John 17:17b; 1 Peter 1:25a

9) Luke 12:4, 5

"He who is greedy for gain troubles his own house,
but he who hates bribes will live."

I had often driven a load of airfreight into this West African airport, but never before had I seen someone stopping vehicles along the airport's main entrance road. Yet there he was, a soldier in khaki uniform with a rifle slung over his shoulder. He was motioning for me to pull over. When I did, he came to my driver's door window. "You need to pay me something to get into the airport," he said. My reply was, "For that you will have to give me a proper receipt." He told me he had none and if I would not give him payment, I would just have to remain there by the roadside. In light of this stalemate, I did what I usually do when confronted with a challenge – I said a quick, silent prayer. Believing he was extorting money from people by his unauthorized actions, I decided to challenge him. I told him I was a God fearing person whose holy book, The Bible, said what he is doing is wrong and for this reason I could not encourage him with payment. It was obvious he did not like me saying that. Just then, an approaching VW Beetle drew his attention away from me. He moved to stop it. Going to the vehicle's passenger side, he exchanged a few words with the car's occupants, then reached his right hand in through a window. When he stepped back the VW took off toward the airport. Returning directly to me, he waved a bill of ill-gotten gain in my face and barked, "And I'm not going to do this! And I'm not going to do this!" He said it twice, as though to emphasize he thought I was crazy to think that he should not do it. After all, wasn't the evidence justifying his doing it right there in his hand? No, it wasn't, not so far as God is concerned.[1]

So I replied, "No, it is wrong for you to demand it and it is wrong for them to give it to you." Now he looked at me like a bull whose nose ring had just been pulled out. Sounding a little like one too, he commanded me to leave. Fortunately, his hand was wildly motioning in the direction of the airport. Thank God, the airfreight was delivered at neither the expense of his conscience or mine.[2]

Lord, grant me wisdom to steer clear of questionable involvements.

1) 1 Cor.6:10b

2) 2 Corinthians 4:2

"The serpent deceived me, and I ate."

It's sad. There are so many broken hearts and homes. Sociologists and psychologists give some ideas as to the reason why. Breakdown of the nuclear family, economic woes, changing cultural norms, early childhood trauma are a few. These are of some value in the analysis of problems, but the Bible clearly discloses the ultimate source of all societal demise lies with that old serpent the devil. He has had great success in defacing the image of God in man. God's image in man today can be likened to a beautiful statue defaced and defamed by relentless stone throwing. It has rendered the original image of God in man very hard to see. Satan has been pounding away at this image ever since he threw the first stone at Eve in the Garden of Eden. His "stone throwing his way through history" has had a cumulative effect. So much so that, in many people today, there remains little untouched image for their soul's detractor to target.

One big stone Satan likes to throw is drugs. There is a proper use of drugs, the benefits of which are not the problem. The problem is with the abuse of drugs so prevalent in our day. How much told and untold defacing of the image of God in man have drugs done! But to generalize this is to probably minimize it, so let's bring it closer by a singular example. Consider the following portion of a letter received by a prison inmate...

Hello John,

My pastor gave your letter out and asked if anyone would like to write you. I said that I would. It has been a while since I said I would write, but I have just now found the time. You see, I work very hard and I have a daughter who is a senior in college this year. Plus, I try very hard to take care of things around my home on my own. I am very independent and I don't like to ask anyone for anything.

I have no idea how you landed up in prison and it is none of my business. However, I know about prison life. My brother spent most of his adult years there. I would say off and on since age 16. After a nine year stint he came out. He only lasted about three years. You see, he was addicted to prescription pain meds. He wound up losing his life over his addiction. It was terrible! He burned in a house fire... all for his drugs. He was 48 years young.

I am not saying, "I am perfect," no one is. The only pure person that walked the face of this earth was Jesus. He suffered, he died for your sins. Don't complain about being poor. I was raised "dirt poor." Don't complain about having no one, because you do have someone... His name is Jesus Christ. Do your time — you did the crime. Pray to the Lord for forgiveness. As for now, you have a roof over your head, meals and a place to sleep. Be thankful, pray hard and be strong in Christ. He is the only way! "Be joyful in hope, patient in affliction, faithful in prayer." (Romans 12:12) I will pray for you John. Will you pray for me?" (signed)-Jean

I think we need to pray for both John and Jean.[1] Stone throwing has had its repercussions on all of us.[2] Thank God, He loves to restore His broken image in His people. [3] None of us is exempt from His repair unless we choose to be. [4]

Lord, you are the potter, I am the clay. Restore me in your image.

1) James 5:16

2) 1 Corinthians 15:48a, 49a

3) 1 Corinthians 15:48b, 49b

4) Romans 6:19

Fig Leaf Righteousness *Gen. 3:7b*

"...they sewed fig leaves together."

It was very clever of Adam and Eve to sew fig leaves together to cover up their nakedness. No fabric was available, nor was a Singer sewing machine anywhere to be found. They used what they had at hand, designing and working out fitting problems as they went along. A project this ambitious, for two people, must have taken some time to complete. They probably felt pretty good about it when they were done. Sad though, all that work was for nothing. What they made was only worn a short time before it was replaced with a covering of superior quality and workmanship. The Lord Himself made larger garments, tunics, for each of them.[1] These skin outfits came at the expense of an innocent animal's sacrifice at the hands of the Almighty. When Adam and Eve removed the product of their own labor, God then clothed them with coverings of His own acceptable material and design.

When we seek to hide behind the works that we do,[2] then we, like Adam and Eve, have covered ourselves with a "fig leaf righteousness" unsatisfactory to God. In His sight, the good works that constitute our fig leaves are just "filthy rags" good for discarding.[3] God demands we be covered with something better, something that only He can provide. He gave it to Adam and Eve, and He is ready to give it to everyone who will drop their "fig leaf righteousness." For those who do, He covers them with the righteousness of Christ,[4] whose sacrifice is by His design and satisfies Him. How about you? What are you covered in today? Fig leaves, or Christ's righteousness?

Lord, help me to drop all fig leaf righteousness
so I may be clothed in your righteousness alone.

1) Genesis 3:21

2) Titus 3:4, 5

3) Isaiah 64:6

4) 2 Corinthians 5:21

Father Knows Best

"Hear, my children, the instruction of a father,
and give attention to understanding."

Have you heard it? Perhaps you have thought it yourself. It is a comment sometimes voiced as a criticism, other times expressed as a perplexity over, or at worst an arguing about, what God could do if He wanted to. For instance, someone will say, "If God is so loving and powerful, why doesn't He just end all wars, take away all pain, heal all people, and settle all the world's problems?" It is an irony that God is preparing to do exactly what they want, just not as immediately as the perplexed or perhaps fault finding inquirer desires.

Why is "wait" so often God's immediate response to the longing of our hearts? For one thing, in regard to everything, our heavenly Father knows best. The all-knowing God who created us certainly has more knowledge of our situations then we will ever have. Like our earthy fathers, He is more experienced and far better equipped to make important decisions for us... decisions that are in our best interest. As His children, we do well to show Him respect and trust in His timing.[1]

Consider the fact that, although Christ healed people while on earth, He did not singularly command the healing of everyone, everywhere. He could have done it had He chose to. But, contemplate the case of one man crippled since birth who was laid out daily at the temple's gate.[2] Christ would have repeatedly passed by him, yet for some reason He did not heal him. Why not? Now, fast forward... Christ has died, been resurrected, and ascended to heaven. He is nowhere on earth to be seen. Then, one Sabbath day, Paul and Silas are headed to the same temple, seeing the same crippled man, the one who was daily laid at the gate Jesus often passed. This day, using Peter as His instrument, Jesus does heal the crippled man.[3] Why now and not before? The grand result of Peter's healing the man in the name of Jesus is the reasonable answer. Because of this miracle, 5000 men who heard Peter's accompanying speech were saved![4] In God's wisdom the man's healing was timed to coincide with the visit of Peter and Silas to the temple that day. The miracle authenticated their message. It gave evidence to the fact that the power behind them was of God.

God has a plan and He is working it. His ways and timing do not include doing things the way people think He should. He is far too wise to require our input. He knows the things we don't so, when it comes to what He does and when He does it, He looks for our trust – not our advice.[5] One day He will see to it that all our pain and sorrows do cease,[6] but until then, like Paul and Silas, we have work to do.[7]

Lord, help me wait patiently for your timely
answers to my longing heart.

1) 2 Peter 3:3-10   4) Acts 4:4

2) Acts 3:1-10   5) Isaiah 40:13

3) Acts 3:16   6) Revelation 21:4   7) Acts 1:8

"We esteemed Him stricken, smitten by God and afflicted."

A mining company has responsibility to maintain use of a retractable railway over a gorge where they have work in progress. The facility's operator manages the spans movement from a building on a nearby hill. Housed within the building's basement are the giant gears which turn to shift and extend the railway span out and across the deep chasm of the gorge.

One beautiful day, the railway operator brought his little son with him to work. He sat him on his own chair, introduced him to coworkers and gave him a tour of the workplace. As was his habit, when the time came for a passenger train to pass through, the father gave attention to writing the date, time and train name in his ledger. After he did, he turned to invite his son to punch the button which would extend the railway. He was immediately alarmed – the boy was nowhere to be seen! Urgently his eyes scanned the room, his heart stopping as he saw an open trap door to the gear room below. Running, he looked into it. There he saw his worst fear... below was his little son, unconscious, with his body entangled in the huge gears. Shock engulfed him. Screaming within himself, he had only a moment to make his choice. He could take time to save his son and let a speeding railroad train with hundreds of souls pass on to die in a wreck or, he could press the button that would crush his son, but save the train. With tears nearly blinding his eyes, he lunged for the button. The train was saved.

In the aftermath of the tragedy, the son was buried and the family grieved. The operator knew the passengers on board the train that day had been talking, sleeping, eating, reading, at the time of his son's sacrifice. They were totally unaware of what had happened. He decided to do something about it. Using the passenger list, he wrote to inform all who had been aboard of what had happened that eventful day. Many of them he never heard from, but from some he did. They said they would never forget his or his son's sacrifice and added that their own lives would never be the same.

One eventful day in history the Lamb of God, God's Son, Jesus Christ, died so that mankind might live. Many people pass on, unaware or indifferent to His and His Father's sacrifice... but some who read and hear believe, and their lives are never the same.

Lord, let me never take you or your Father's sacrifice for granted.

"Who is the King of glory?
The LORD strong and mighty, the LORD mighty in battle."

Our God is a warrior. He is experienced in battle. See Him in the wilderness where He successfully counters the schemes of the devil,[1] at the cross where He defeats sin,[2] or at the tomb where He overcomes the pangs of death.[3] Our God is a warrior. See Him returning to make war as the "Lion of Judah."[4] He does it with His armies of heaven.[5] Our God is a warrior. His descriptive titles testify to this truth. He is "shield,"[6] "defender,"[7] "strong tower,"[8] "fortress,"[9] and "Lord of Hosts."[10] Yes, our God is a warrior and He makes His followers warriors too.

See David and his mighty men battling the armies of their enemies,[11] Gideon and his few defeating overwhelming odds, [12] or Elijah's victory in his confrontation with those who opposed God on Mount Carmel.[13] Look at Samson. When the Spirit of the Lord came upon him, he alone killed a thousand of the enemy.[14] Yes, our God is a warrior and He makes His followers warriors too. Today, the same "warrior spirit" needs to be yours. Whoever you are, the Lord knows you need victories over your soul's enemies - the world, the flesh, and the devil. Because God knows your frailty, He wants to give Himself to you as a refuge and rock,[15] a fortress of defense to which you can run.[16] What's more, He wants to give you His own protective armor to put on.[17] Your learning how to use such assets is part of his "training your hands to war"[18] so that, like other soldiers before you, in your time of combat, you may "run through a troop or leap over a wall."[19] If you take this call to battle seriously, you will prepare yourself to be alert to enemy ambush so you will not be taken by surprise... for "your adversary the devil, as a roaring lion, walks about, seeking who he may devour."[20]

Soldier, inspect your armor and put it on daily.[21] Stay in sight of your fortress and run to Him as often as necessary. Remember, your God is a warrior and He would have you be a warrior too.[22]

Lord, thank you for being my fortress and providing me protection.

Teach me to be a warrior. I want to be victorious for you.

1) Matthew 4:1-10

2) Colossians 2:13-15

3) 1 Corinthians 15:54

4) Revelation 19:11

5) Revelation 19:14

6) Genesis 5:1

7) Psalm 89:18

8) Psalm 61:3

9) Psalm 18:2

10) Psalm 24:10

11) 1 Chronicles 12

12) Judges 7

13) 1 Kings 18:1-39

14) Judges 15:13-15

15) Psalm 62:7

16) Psalm 18:10

17) Ephesians 6:11

18) Psalm 18:34

19) Psalm 18:29

20) 1 Peter 5:8

21) Ephesians 6:13-17

22) 2 Timothy 2:3

Works by L. R. Abbott

ONE MAN'S JOURNEY

What does a Christian life look like? The author offers his own up in example. Not that his life is just like yours, but the spiritual truths God teaches him apply to your journey.   Come with him on a pilgrimage reminiscent of the one made by Pilgrim, the main character in John Bunyan's immortal classic Pilgrim's Progress. On the way to the Celestial City, Pilgrim did not avoid every pitfall, and neither did the author. What about you? Have you ever strayed, ever failed to stay on the right path?   Confirm you are on the right path.   Find strength for your pilgrimage and get to where you want to arrive... read One Man's Journey.

THE MONTH THAT MATTERS SERIES

A MONTH THAT MATTERS
ANOTHER MONTH THAT MATTERS
ONE MORE MONTH THAT MATTERS

If you enjoyed this volume of A Month That Matters, you will also enjoy the other volumes of evangelical essays and prayers written for your heart and mind. Each presents a unique set of writings, one for each day of the month. None are too long not to be read in one sitting, but none is too short to be shallow. Take yourself out of yourself for a few minutes each day and read more of The Month That Matters series... you will be glad you did.

ABOUT THE AUTHOR

L. R. Abbott's secular studies earned him a B.S. In Sociology with a minor in English. To prepare for teaching Sociology in colleges he attended graduate school at the New School for Social Research in New York City. There, disillusioned with his search for the answer to life's meaning, he quit his studies and became a practitioner and advocate of Transcendental Meditation. Eventually he met Christ and nothing was the same. In the ensuing years his hunger for spiritual knowledge led him to attend, or complete by extension, classes and courses from Moody Bible Institute, Philadelphia College of the Bible, the Central Jersey Bible Institute and Columbia International University. Now retired, he lives in Columbia, South Carolina.

The author may be contacted at OMJAbbott@yahoo.com

Made in the USA
Columbia, SC
07 November 2023

25629174R00041